Dwelling
an ecopoem

Dwelling

an ecopoem

Dear Michelle —
Dwell in possibility,
as the poet says —
SEA
August
2019

Scott Edward Anderson

Shanti Arts Publishing
Brunswick, Maine

Dwelling: an ecopoem

Published by Shanti Arts Publishing

Interior and cover design by Shanti Arts Designs

Shanti Arts LLC
193 Hillside Road
Brunswick, Maine 04011
shantiarts.com

Printed in the United States of America

Cover image by Hans Van Meeuwen, *14A304*, 2004.
Pencil on paper. Used with permission of the artist.
Interior images by Hans Van Meeuwen, (in order of
appearance) *33A411*, 2011; *31A411*, 2011; and *20A309*,
2009. Pencil on paper. Used with permission of the artist.

ISBN: 978-1-947067-50-9 (print)
ISBN: 978-1-947067-51-6 (digital)

LCCN: 2018957150

for Alison Hawthorne Deming,
who challenged and encouraged me to dwell in this work

&

for Samantha,
together we've turned our "oneiric house" into a home — f, c & a

also by

Scott Edward Anderson

Fallow Field

Walks in Nature's Empire

"Perhaps this attempt to think about dwelling and building will bring out somewhat more clearly that building belongs to dwelling and how it receives its nature from dwelling. Enough will have been gained if dwelling and building have become worthy of questioning and thus have remained worthy of thought."

— MARTIN HEIDEGGER, from "Building Dwelling Thinking"

"Important lessons: look carefully; record what you see. Find a way to make beauty necessary; find a way to make necessity beautiful."

— ANNE MICHAELS, from *Fugitive Pieces*

"Even when a journey seems no distance at all, it can have no return."

— ITALO CALVINO, from *The Baron in the Trees*

"A sustainability revolution requires each person to act as a learning leader at some level, from family to community to nation to the world."

— DONELLA MEADOWS, from *Beyond the Limits*

"There exists for each one of us an oneiric house, a house of dream-memory, that is lost in the shadow beyond the real past."

— GASTON BACHELARD, from *The Poetics of Space*

Contents

TWO — Some Questions of Dwelling
(and the nature of the ecopoem)

Acknowledgments

Grateful acknowledgment to the editors of the following publications, in which the corresponding poems appeared:

Bolts of Silk: "Cultivating (Preserving)"; *CrossConnect*: "Indwelling" and "Running"; *Elegant Thorn Review*: "Healing"; *Many Mountains Moving*: "Presencing"; *Poetica*: "Dwelling: to take leave"; *Terrain: A Journal of the Built and Natural Environments*: "Redshifting," "Shapeshifting," "Mapping," "Bridging," and "Bridging 2 (Gathering)"; *The Wayfarer*: "Embracing," "Savoring," "Surfacing," and "Wondering"

Dwelling: an ecopoem received an Honorable Mention for The Hopper Poetry Prize in 2017 and a few of the poems previously appeared in the author's book *Fallow Field* (Aldrich Press, 2013).

Several of the poems in this sequence premiered in a reading at the Association for the Study of Literature & Environment (ASLE) Conference: "Species, Space, and the Imagination of the Global," Indiana University, Bloomington, Indiana, June 2011.

"Becoming" appeared on a glass wall display at the Millay Colony for the Arts, 30th Anniversary Exhibit, Albany International Airport Gallery, selected by John Ashbery, January through August 2004.

A selection of "Some Questions of Dwelling (and the nature of the ecopoem)" benefited greatly by suggestions from two editorial reviewers for the journal *ISLE: Interdisciplinary Studies in Literature and Environment*. While the selection ultimately did not appear in publication, the author wishes to express his gratitude for their assistance in improving and updating this work. Special thanks to the Concordia Foundation and the Millay Colony for the Arts in Austerlitz, New York, which provided the author with time and space to write this book in an inspirational landscape back in November 2002, and to the author's former colleagues at The Nature Conservancy for a sabbatical at that time and for inspiring him to strive for a world where people and nature thrive.

One

Dwelling: A Poem Sequence

Becoming

Say that childhood memory
has more relevance than yesterday —

a moose calf curled up against the side of a house

merely saying it may make it so.

The way a sunflower towers over a child,
each year growing shorter —

a hermit crab crawling out of a coconut

or no, the child growing taller.

Naming the childhood memory
bears witness to his knowing —

a hawk swooping over a stubble field

imagining the earth, "the earth is all before me,"
blossoming as it stretches to the sun —

a red eft held aloft in a small, pink hand

Is home the mother's embrace?

a cabbage butterfly flitting from flower tops

Do we carry home within?

The child sees his world or hers

stroking the "furry" back of a bumblebee

Dwelling: to linger — Linger there, in the arms of your lover as

head full of seed, until it droops,

spent, ready to sow the seeds of its own becoming,
say that our presence in the world

a millipede curling up at the slightest touch

is in making the book of our becoming.

the dawn stretches her rose-red fingers — don't be so quick to

Surfacing

If this were the beginning of a poem, he would have called the
thing he felt inside him the silence of snow. — Orhan Pamuk

The sound of the stream as it fills and flows
— under a full moon and stars — with melting snow.

The sound of your breathing as it fills and furls
in early winter air beneath the pines.

Say that the flow of a stream is surfacing a *langscape*,
surfacing the stream: shushing shushing susurrus

within you responding —

The way a crow responds to another,
as it dreams of the road kill over the ridge.

The way deer browse for succulent shoots
or a dream of deer, hooving under surface.

Say that air flows around objects as a stream around rock,
surfacing the stream: leaves plastering color to surface

of a half-submerged stone —

jump up and make excuses, to run out the door, get into your

Shapeshifting

When young Dawn with her rose-red fingers shone once more . . . — Homer

Give the night back to the night,
the stars back to the sky —

Give the earth, spinning in space,
back to the earth —

(the stars look black tonight)

Give the moon, no, keep the moon,
it is the stars we want to give back —

Give the soil back to the isopod
emerging to the surface

(what is it looking for?)

Give the Dawn back her rose-red fingers,
she needs them more than the night.

Give the blue jay back his morning,
taken from him by the chickadee —

(sounds are deeper in solitude)

Give back to the sunshine
what darkness is his —

Give back to the night
what light is hers —

(stars, moon, clouds —)

car and drive up the road out of the canyon. You may regret it

Shape-shifting: blue jay into chickadee
into blue jay, night into day

into — what?

          ("harassed unrest"?)

Give back to the Earth what is hers,
she will forgive you for taking it

          or she will turn into a wolf.

later, not lingering, the pillow talk and possibly more . . . What

Savoring

*Sometimes I think this, our life on earth, is an egg to
break out of.* — Susan Mitchell

Watch the birds grow full with bursting
spring. Rapacious bees come from nowhere

covering themselves in pollen, until
they are loaded with murky pastel —

humid, torpid, full with desire only
to be laden, to be laid in humid dust.

Take the pollen on your fingers, rub
two fingers together, make an oil-pastel

of pollen and rub it over your eyelids.
Now go to your lover, your "bee's knees,"

and close your eyes.

Sun-drenched, the garden grows fecund
in the naming earth — in a few days

the peonies will be two-feet tall and laden
with black ants, sucking the swelling buds —

sap runs, and the garden grows green,
then pink, blue, white, yellow, purple.

Ochre pollen covers the porch deck
and rail — pollen does not discriminate,

except flower to flower, sinus to sinus,
as the trees give out their leafy life.

falls between two people or what two people befall, caught in

Redshifting

Everything, even size, is a human value . . . miniature is
vast in its way. — Gaston Bachelard

A crow makes its call from a distant tree,
rain soaking the meadow, soaking the earth.

Say that surfacing on the wind is as an oak leaf
cutting through air —

The way the universe expands in space-time,
with little regard for the matter in its way —

A star in the night sky redshifting (did you see it?)
as the eye adjusts, from blue to green to yellow to red.

An object radiates light, moving away from us,
lightwaves becoming longer, less energetic,

red heart pulsing, wavelength of lower frequency
then blue heart, pulsing out longing —

The crow flies overhead, cawing, its frequency,
its pitch, becoming higher when approaching,

then lower, longer, as it passes, until distance
makes the heart's pitch lower, too, with absence.

Absence being a lower frequency than presence —
Say that the heart redshifts down

as it reflects light, distance being
the time it takes love to travel from star to star,

the wind, as it blows against the sails. Like Odysseus opening

22

lover to loved. Love is not a vacuum,
its waves bend with its expansion,

the heart is as that red star in a field
of blue; we cannot know its origin or

its destination — but if we think about that place,
or that absence, we are already there

redshifting through the distance of space-time or
blueshifting, where frequency and proximity collide.

his ears to the Siren's calls, lashed to the mast he cannot

Breathing

Out of this same light, out of the central mind/ we make a dwelling in the
evening air,/ in which being there together is enough. —Wallace Stevens

I.

Anticipation, the bounce in your step
as you go to her, take her in your arms

and lift her — the way her weight disappears
as you carry her to the bed, lay her down,

begin unclothing, playing fingers
over skin, caressing shoulders, parting hair,

or that moment before plunging headlong into pungent love smell,
scent of anticipation, scent of adrenaline —

it's the same scent that lingers
at the base of her neck, where her hair flows

down where it meets the skin —
the folds of her body enfolding you,

bird wings drum in your ear, *Doppler distance,*
or the beat of the earth, *intimately distant* —

and you breathe in that scent, holding onto it,
like a river holds a leaf as it contours a landscape.

II.

As a child, you dreamed (or maybe
it wasn't a dream) that you could dive into the earth,

move — imploring, imploring, entreating, not retreating —

swim through soil, through leaf litter, detritus
humus — *mor* or *mull*, no matter — fungi, tiny organisms,

isopods and bacteria — busy biomass,
and you swam deep into the soil of the forest floor,

you could breathe and your breath was full
of soil — pungent earth smell — and so it is

with love, diving deep
into the soil and breathing it all in,

until the body lets go of its *otherness*, no longer
apart from but *a part of* —

until presence is felt in absence
and what lingers is that scent of adrenaline,

of anticipation, and that *frisson*, firing or frying
the neurons of memory, and you hold it close

with you, for those moments when life
leaves you stranded, resolutely

human — *dour* or *dull*. November trees soaked with rain,
leaves fallen to the forest floor, wildflowers

spent, the last bees and wasps gasping
for their last breaths, if breathing is what they do,

and the sound of her breathing
sinks you deep in her earth, brings you home.

Dwelling: to lead astray —   "Don't go there," says the

Presencing

I.

A space must be maintained or desire ends. — Anne Carson

The scent of your presence evaporates desire,
the space between you and we, between otherness —

becoming the presence of another's absence;
weight of earth spinning its matter apart, weight

of our *becoming*, our *presencing*.
At present, the time between past and future —

"this very time that is space, this very space that is time." (Merleau-Ponty)
Vanishing space that surrounds us, space of intimacy;

a collarbone caressed by a tongue, hair flowing over hipbones —
scent of your presence lingering, trapping memory in a lifetime,

an infinite solitude. Solitude the presence of absence:
scent of a fox long after the fox is gone —

II.

True love lives in absence . . . — John Clare

Presence, essence, *esse, in esse*: in view.
Absence, *abesse*: to be away.

abesse, esse, interesse: absence leads to interest in presence, hence desire

> of a lover
> of another
> of an *Other*

Muse. "You may never return." Still, you go, and you

of one
of you

of what one holds near
nearness
holds dear
dearness
abesse
absence
desir

desiderāre: to regret the absence of, not to regress,
go back, but to regret, to re-greet

(to greet again?).

III.

The nearness of you
evaporates absence,
as presence evaporates absence,
essence remains, hence desire —
your presencing becomes
your absence, your essence.

cannot regret all that's about to happen. Neither can

Longing

Love is the distance | between you and what you love
|| what you love is your fate — Frank Bidart

Desire is a city street flush with longing;
losing is the darkness inhabiting that street.

Say that losing becomes a way of knowing,
words failing to capture its music —

Desire is to longing as longing is to losing.
If this is so, losing strengthens longing

as longing makes mystery of desire.
Concave mirrors cascading light in common focus

each reflecting and magnifying the other,
unformed or uninformed, but nevertheless —

Life's little endings: the big unresolved, unrequited
unfolding of the world into what longing desires.

you predict the direction of what leads you — to the

Indwelling

Shooting stars cross a city sky. In the moment
before they fall, think about dwellings,

houses made of brick, stone, and wood — dwelling and indwelling —
miracle keeping matter together, from imploding or inverting.

How dwellings become a city, interdependent.
How stars become a night sky, suspended.

*(Late Fall, nearly winter, fog-caul warms night air through inversion.
The meteor version of life heads straight to the matter of our bed.)*

What holds up the sky holds each one of us, too —
as we move against one another in this taut, elastic field,

warming with each movement, causing little inversions
all around us, and shooting stars —

there goes another.

left: a canyon to the right: a forest. Which will it be? You

Dwelling

I.

Bridges and factories,
supermarkets and box stores,
airports and power stations
are buildings, not dwellings.

Train stations and breweries,
office parks and dams,
malls, stadiums, and concert halls
are built, but are not dwelling places.

The truck driver is "at home"
on the Interstate,
or the truck stop,
but he seeks no shelter there.

The CEO finds comfort
in the boardroom,
but she does not
make her dwelling there.

*(These buildings "house" human beings.
We inhabit them, yet we do not dwell in them.)*

II.

To dwell: to remain,
to tarry in a place;
learning a place, intimately,
is a form of dwelling.

go the way the Fates lead you — taking chances and

Thinking about dwelling
is being human.
"I dwell therefore I am."
Dwelling means being part of
(not apart from) nature.

We are insofar as we dwell.
Building as dwelling is "habitual."
Do we dwell out of habit
or because dwelling is what we do?

Inhabitants seek home,
more than just buildings
that are habitable.
Dwelling *is* habitation.

III.

We inhabit,
we inhabit the earth,
we inhabit a habitat,
we inhabit a building,
we inhabit a dwelling,
we are in habit.

We do not dwell because we build;
we build because
we dwell.
We dwell *because*
we are dwellers;
we are insofar as we dwell.
Home inhabits you.

making choices along the way — Where will we go today?

Saving

> But where danger is, grows | The saving power
> also ... — Frederich Hölderlin

Saving means to snatch from danger,
to remove threats and stem loss.
Saving means setting aside
from things that endanger.

Say that saving is more
than sparing and preserving;
it is caching for the future,
forestalling use.

To save also means cultivating,
setting things free.
To save means leaving something
to its own devices, preserved for itself alone.

Earth is the habit we wear,
the provider, provender —
"grounded" in rock and water,
fulfilling itself in plants and animals.

To be stewards of the earth means
to take it under one's care,
to look after, to spare and preserve,
to protect from harm.

Dwelling: to take leave —   The Poet says leave-taking is

Cultivating

I.

The gardener removes
that which inhibits growth.

If certain plants need fire,
the gardener introduces fire.

If other plants need more nitrogen,
the gardener adds more nitrogen.

Plants that require distance
from other plants are moved away.

Removing some species from a habitat,
the gardener removes what inhibits growth.

(Not "survival of the fittest," but survival
of right relationship to place.)

II.

Dwelling as preserving
is cultivating.
Dwelling means knowing
what inhabits a place
and understanding that
which *belongs* to a place.

We cultivate what grows,
while building things
that don't grow.
We seek the organic

the hardest part: withdrawal, saying goodnight, parting,

in our own creations,
which are inorganic.

Imposing our will
on the landscape,
we can remove either
that which promotes capacity
or that which prevents capacity.

We are tenders of the garden,
we tend what needs tending
(heart or "langscape")
What we save remains —

saying goodbye, longing to stay but knowing to let go, to

Healing

Healing, not saving. — Gary Snyder

"Healing, not saving," for healing
indicates corrective, reclaiming

restoring the earth to its bounty,
to right placement and meaning—

Forward thinking, making things new
or better or, at least, bringing back

from the edge. The way
bulbs are nestled in earth,

starting to heal again—
the way a wound heals.

Keep warm. Sun following
rain; rain following drought.

Perhaps we have come far enough
along in this world to start

healing, protecting from harm,
from our disjunctive lives.

The way the skin repairs with a scab,
injury mediated by mindfulness.

The bark of the "tree of blood"
heals wounds we cannot see.

Deliver us from the time of trial
and save us from ourselves.

take leave is the being of dwelling. That which we hold

Mapping

More delicate than the historians' are the
map-makers' colors. — Elizabeth Bishop

A boundary is where something begins,
spaces formed by locations.
Mapping is building spaces
and locations, as it is made.

Nature's boundaries
defined by interconnections,
and geophysical fact
not geopolitical friction —

Aspect, climate, elevation,
land forms and bodies of water,
aggregation of species,
watershed divides,
soil, time, bedrock, strata,
and shifting —

of this we are certain:
boundaries are always shifting.
(Only Man tries to deny this,
imposing order where chaos rules.)

Say that boundaries
are the beginning,
where things start,
not the end-point;
say boundaries are a beginning,
one among many.

most dear must be set free, the Philosopher argues; still,

Mapping delineates spaces
and locations through form.
Each boundary,
while defining the end
of shaped space,
is also a beginning.

the Poet longs for the past, keeping an eye on the future

Building

Architecture is a society's unbribable witness.
— Octavio Paz

The making of things is building.
Building is founding and joining spaces.

Technē: to bring forth or produce.
The nature of building is letting dwell.

Can the architect find locations,
to bring forth dwelling?

Building accomplishes its nature
by joining spaces through locations.

Building produces locations,
the way earth and sky come together.

Building is letting dwell;
dwelling requires thinking.

Architects build out of dwelling;
think for the sake of dwelling.

When we build without thinking,
we cannot accomplish dwelling.

Without thinking, building merely fills spaces,
inexorably, within locations; think:

"Location, location, location"
and *"There is no there there."*

and trying to live in the moment even when it's time to go.

If we build with thinking,
with dwelling as purpose,

buildings give form to dwelling
and house its presence.

Dwelling: to tarry —   Stay awhile at this bar table,

Housing

The houses of our memories abide us.
Those lost or never owned,
those only desired sweep up
into our senses, becoming dreamable.

We see the old, creaky lakeside house
with the same eyes as the new house
in the woods; the family house retaining
memories, a tincture of envy.

These are not our houses.
Our houses are on city streets,
in neighborhoods back before memory.
These houses inhabit dreams before we had a house.

The houses of our memories abide us.
Stoking fires, warming the night of the earth
our fractured, fragile home.
How we dwell takes shape before our birth.

How we dwell upon the earth
is how we are *housed* — homes inhabit
our memories, forsaking what happens within.
We abide those memories that abide us.

Our desires make the house we hold;
our longing breathes life into *home*.
We make of our houses what we will.
We make beds of our houses and lie in them,

never unquestioning memory.

linger over a beer or two and some heady conversation.

Emerging

*The universe is a communion and a community. We ourselves
are that communion become conscious of itself.* — Thomas Berry

I.

Just as the stream, as if yielding to remembrance,
seems to measure back the way it came,

so we have made motions to return,
to emerge into the patterns or our dwelling.

Say that emerging is a coming together
in common purpose, communion.

A community emerges to form a neighborhood,
people coming together to form a community.

We are part of the earth's community,
we are part of an ever-renewing process of emerging.

II.

Our community is our bioregion and all its components,
organic and inorganic, culture and nature.

Our communities are a communion in holding
something in common — purpose, place, dwelling.

Our communion is a sharing with each other:
to commune, to render available to all, to have in common.

Our communities emerge as we commune together,
sharing the place of our dwelling.

Let's talk of poetry and music, of poets who took

Running

Not beauty, or ugliness, either, but a disturbing kind of satisfaction.
— Philip Johnson

Think of a watershed as a river's neighborhood;
the running stream, a kind of architecture —

Find the stream that forms the watershed in which you live;
hear the water running (if it is frozen, listen through the ice).

The architect finds such harmony
in the precise moment a corner is designed —
tension, productivity, and grace.

Hear it?
Running water, then silence, then water running.

The architect Frank Gehry achieves
a "double sense of space"; like a watershed,
his buildings are formed by what flows in *and* out —

Follow the stream, run the watershed,
chase the flash-and-glamour of fish scales
underwater: spawning entire new dynamics of space.

The way a storm moving through a valley
redirects energy back into a stream.

Gehry asked himself, "Why not do fish?"
A lasting design, form linked to function.

So he did fish. Fish scale chairs, fish lamps.
And then buildings, buildings
that seemed to swim around their own corners, seemed to spawn.

their own lives in rivers or off bridges in other cities.

Scale the banks, river walls, riverrun
— erosion and construction —

titanium trapezoids billowing at the end of Bilbao's streets,
more like spun-sugar than shaped metal.

Run the river toward *something*.
There's tension in productivity and grace.

Perhaps this double sense of space is sense of place:
No matter where we are, we are always in a watershed

Let's ponder Heidegger's dilemma or the dilemma

Dwelling (ecos)

How do we begin building the place of our dwelling?

With
stones
wood
brick
concrete
adobe
earth
stories
poems
memory
mystery

eco (*oikos*): of the household, dwelling-place
economy (*oikonomia*): household management
ecology (*oikologia*): household environment
oikein: to inhabit
oikoumenē: the inhabited world
oikonomos: steward
paraoikia: a sojourning
ecophobia: a dread of home

Is there no building whose essence is not dwelling?
Bring forth that essence.
Bridge it to our dwelling.

of Heidegger, and stick around until it's time to go.

Bridging

> *Between now and now, between I am and you are, the word bridge.*
> — Octavio Paz

I.

The bridge arcs over the stream
connecting more than just the banks.

The bridge connects water as water
connects the banks. They begin to emerge
as the bridge crosses the stream.

The bridge brings together
the expanse of landscape
extending beyond each bank —

Water may drift beneath the bridge
or be lathered by floods.

The bridge is braced for the sky and weather.
Ice floes move under the bridge the way life flows.

II.

The city bridge connects commerce
with marketplace, exchanging goods and ideas.

The old stone bridge crosses an unassuming brook,
providing passage from field to village.

The floating bridge brings enlightenment to Pliny's raven —
weight crossing displaces water determining volume.

Dwelling: to wander — Searching the world over for home or

The highway bridge creates a long-distance network,
making "remote" seem obsolete.

The suspension bridge proves nothing about human ingenuity,
only that tension combs strength from chaos.

The covered bridge is a repository for memory,
yet neither building nor dwelling.

The bridge between two people is *within* two people,
the way a river flows without acknowledging the bridge—

Bridges connect and combine, cross and current,
the way words connect lovers over distance and time.

something like the idea of home — What is home to one who

Embracing

Longing for home is the desire for love,
as desire for love is longing for security.

If this is so, our need for love
is as compelling as our need for food —

Can dwelling fulfill this need by sustaining
our need for love, for security?

Our attraction conjures energy,
holding matter together.

Energy between two people is
frisson, bodies of energy and mass

colluding and colliding and sparking —
desiring, longing, dwelling.

Atoms coalescing, mass tugging and pulling,
coming together even as it moves apart —

Electrical charges pulling and pulsing
drawing together or being repulsed.

Trees and plants may hold the vestiges
of love, Erasmus asserts,

the "vine embraces the elm, other plants
cling to the vine," desiring union.

We hold fast in embrace, "the attraction of cohesion,"
embracing all nature in nature's embrace.

Embracing enacts the law of love;
love of nature is embracing our dwelling on earth.

has never known home? Constantly wandering from place

Wondering

Enough of longing, spent desires
come quickly to the new spring —

Busy anthills, first bees,
nests being built by furtive

mothers or mothers-to-be — they grow larger
with the coming spring, full to bursting,

as busy bodies from within —
("the fecundity factor")

tensile skin of the flower bed,
flap-down-drawn doodle of pollen;

warblers have yet to return,
but their song explodes all around

leaving us to wonder,
to wander in our own way.

to place, searching for a place to call his own. He wanders

Forgetting

How to speak a "forgotten language"
to write for those beings that have no writing

> *a doe taken down by coyotes on the yard-thick ice of a January pond*

to make "beauty necessary . . . to make necessity beautiful"
to seek forgiveness in a lover's eyes

> *water evaporating from a vernal pool*

to imagine a world without forgetting
to protect the earth, our only home

> *a snake in the Sierra Nevada swallows a meadow vole; its last meal*

to forget the way her hair fell, overflowing
to interpret birdsong in the air

> *a fox runs off after being rescued from an empty swimming pool*

to love this world
to render unto Caesar what is his

> *a kestrel nails a sparrow in a chain-link fence*

how to believe in something
how to behave at the dinner table

> *a teenage boy kills a girl while cleaning a hunting rifle*

to forget where you came from
to unlearn all that must be unlearned

the world over, the "ranting rover," from hillside to the

Galapágos land iguana spitting under a bush;
only the marine iguana is more hideous

to speak for the trees
to make mistakes, to be in error

the way a gust of wind lifts a tent aloft

how to think about forgetting,
to remember all that has already been forgotten —

white cliffs of Dover. ("Can you believe he trotted out that

Bridging 2 (Gathering, an "ecologue")

Say that the bridge is a location,
the way a bridge brings together the banks of a river —

(Okay, the bridge gathers . . .)

There are many spaces along the river
that can be occupied by *something*.

(Something, anything . . . ?)

One of these spaces proves to be a location
and does so because of the bridge.

(So Heidegger asserts . . .)

Say that the bridge does not come to be a location,
but location comes into being by virtue of the bridge —

(Do we really agree with that?)

The way points on a map are described by naming, by symbols;
the way mapping becomes an organized presencing.

(Shall we gather at the river . . .)

When we speak of human beings and space
we do not mean human beings on one side,

(The river, the beautiful river . . .)

space on the other —
The bridge gathers, uniting the banks of our river.

(Our beautiful, beautiful river . . .)

one? You can almost hear him singing . . . ") He cannot stop

Wanting

If you put up a wall, think what's left outside!
— Italo Calvino

We need a culture
of different wants.

By creating a second nature,
do we separate ourselves from nature?

"Nature" describes an idea
derived from sensory experience.

(When you read *nature*, what do you see?)

The written text, a portable homeland;
a poem is a tree as much as its paper.

Make a poetry of *langscape*,
make it all about desire.

until he finds his home — there, the one with the light on.

"When the forest falls silent / The forest speaks on."

— Fernando Pessoa

"'Questioning means taking the road to despair,' continued the second disciple. 'We will never know what we are trying to learn.'"

— Edmund Jabès, from *The Book of Questions*

Two

Some Questions of Dwelling
(and the nature of the ecopoem)

The Question of "Nature"

Rousseau defined nature as an innate disposition or inherent constitution — not only that with which we are born, but also that which we develop in response to our infant and childhood environment. "Nature" can be all the phenomena of the material world or the earth's features, as opposed to merely those associated only with humanity.

Philosopher Kate Soper, in her book *What is Nature?: Culture, Politics and the non-Human*, offers a threefold articulation:

1. the concept of the non-human;
2. the structures, processes, and causal powers that are constantly operative within the physical world;
3. the nature of immediate experience and aesthetic appreciation.

Soper remarks that "even Cicero distinguished between an inherited non-human nature and a nature constructed through human activity . . . 'one may say that we seek with our human hands to create a *second nature* in the natural world.'"

In creating a second nature, do we not set up a distinction or separation between human beings and the rest of nature? We become *apart from* rather than *a part of* nature, denying the part of us — biology — that links us to the rest of nature, to the non-human. Our technology furthers this separation, keeping us at arm's length — or even the infinity found within a silicon chip — from nature.

But in denying nature and contributing to that separation, whether from the physical environment or the non-human, we are attempting to elevate human beings to the status of a sort of "super-species." Do

---

Dwelling: to abandon —   Abandoning hope for the eternal

we assume, then, that we are *above* nature? What is the "nature" of such a conundrum? There are, no doubt, unintended consequences of such an assumption, some of which create a dichotomy that will have lasting impact on our species' future. (Consider climate change and our failure to act upon it.)

As we further separate ourselves from nature and somehow become super-Nature, we end up distancing ourselves from ourselves, from our true nature.

The unintended consequences of such distancing can include, but are not limited to, hubris, solipsism, consumerism, escapism, pedantry, idolatry (of things human and human-made), and self-adoration.

If taken to the extreme, we can wall ourselves off from Nature in the way a gated community walls itself off from "undesirables," but in essence locks us in and makes us more remote from one another and, eventually, from ourselves.

dwelling, the Poet looks inward, while others look

The Question of Language

Technology separates us from nature. The pen with which we write is an instrument for translating experience into words. Perhaps the instrument and language itself causes this separation. Human beings experience the world mediated by language. It is difficult to do otherwise. Perhaps this is our true nature, fostering a dynamic relationship — an interrelationship — between the earth and its apprehension by the mind. A Cartesian dualism contributes to the gulf between human and non-human, between human and nature. In other words, we are somehow "separate" because we are "language-users."

We developed language to communicate with others of our species; however, we use the same language with our domestic pets — cats, dogs, horses, etc. — as if these animals somehow understand our language. We make these select animals more "like us" through our relationships with them. Indeed, many of them share our homes and even our beds. It's amazing that these animals have failed to become language-users. "If we could talk to the animals . . . "

Our children's literature is full of animals speaking our human languages. In an extreme case, C. S. Lewis's *Narnia Chronicles* features animals speaking our language to such a high degree that human adults cannot comprehend it; only children can understand. This may be "pathetic fallacy" in the extreme, but it speaks volumes about our culture and our nature.

Animal sounds may be a kind of language, a communication. Some primates, monkeys, and gorillas have been shown to "understand" or at least to react to our language. And what about dolphins? Should we allow language to separate us from nature? "If you put up a wall," wrote Italo Calvino in *The Baron in the Trees*, "think what's left outside!"

out   on   the   night   awaiting   this   morning's   transit   of

If language is a freak of nature — and our capacity for language is, as Noam Chomsky asserts, an accident of neural mechanics within the human brain — is it not, therefore, a part of nature? Why then should language contribute to our separation from nature?

Perhaps because it sets up a barrier between us and the thing or being our language describes. We cannot look at something without forming a word for it, if only silently in our minds.

Therefore, we immediately separate ourselves from the object in our sight. Try looking at a tree without thinking, "Tree" or, more concretely, "oak," "maple," or "pine." Try disassociating language from the thing itself and, further, all the associations we have for the word describing that thing.

It is like a wall set up between us that causes this separation. Our words replace the object. Almost, I want to say, our words *become* the object.

Venus. Heavy spring, the goddess of love smiles upon

The Question of Writing

When writing about Nature we describe it; therefore, we are writing from outside, from our experience of the world as an observer. We can never write from within nature because, as human beings, we are the only species to have designed writing tools and language to communicate experience, which, as we've seen, separates us from Nature.

Phenomenologist Gaston Bachelard writes "that the two terms 'outside' and 'inside' pose problems of metaphysical anthropology that are not symmetrical." He goes on to distinguish between the two, with the outside being vast and the inside being concrete. But for Bachelard, the division between the two is not a true division: "everything, even size, is a human value . . . miniature is vast in its way."

So, what of writing? We cannot write from within nature, from inside, if we are already distanced from nature by the instruments we use and by our comprehension. Our "dissociation" from the natural world is a root cause of our species' ability to disregard our dependence upon ecological systems. Indeed, our disregard for the air we breathe or the waters we drink stems from this very dissociation. Even from those things that give us life we are distanced to such a degree that we don't even notice we are despoiling our environment, our only home.

In *The Spell of the Sensuous*, philosopher and magician David Abrams claims that "the civilized mind still feels itself somehow separate, autonomous, independent of the body and bodily nature in general." Only when we immerse ourselves in the experience of the environment around us, Abrams asserts, "do we start to recall what it is to be fully a part of this world."

those who pay her tribute, if they pay to play at all.

Written language contributes to our dissociation, taking us out of the immersion where our senses must interpret information as it is received. Through writing, we process experience inside and catalog it, accumulating knowledge we have gained outside of ourselves. Others experience our experience through our words, not through their bodies.

Nature becomes Other, because nature is not a thing. "Nature" is a word used to describe an idea based upon sensory experience. Nature is a human concept, a construct of our minds.

The scent of a fox lingering in a meadow says "fox" to us as we translate it into words. It is outside us, even while the idea resides within. When we write "Nature," we identify it as outside of ourselves and ourselves outside of it. When you read the word *nature*, what do you see?

Dwelling: to delay — Each point "a delay" from going on,

The Question of Displacement

Displacement is a sort of exile; it comes from *exiliāre*, to drive out, to banish. Our exile from nature has its roots, according to David Abrams, in our use of an alphabet. The alphabet, Abrams argues in *The Spell of the Sensuous*, distances us from the immediate, sensual experience of our world, setting up a barrier between us, limiting direct contact with place. We are constantly interpreting the earth through our language, through our alphabet and its corresponding words.

Abrams conflates the time of the Hebraic people's exodus from Egypt, around 1250 B.C.E., and the development of the aleph-beth, the precursor to our alphabetic system. The Hebrew scribes recorded the cultural and experiential stories of their homeland and exchanged these stories with one another. Away went the oral transmission of such cultural stories and their placement in the land. Now the stories could travel great distances, passing from one person to another, and into the strange and distant lands of their exile.

In exile, the Jews were already separated from experiencing the physical place of their stories, places that had resonance to those who had experienced them. The stories were preserved and probably reached and instructed many more people than if kept orally or locally, but here was a new layer of displacement, the aleph-beth, contributing to a break with the land.

By carrying their stories in written form, they preserved their culture, and "the written text became a kind of portable homeland for the Hebrew people." They carried their homeland with them through ancestral stories while in a continuous state of exile from their grounding. In a sense, they carried their dwelling on their backs.

---

proceeding. Yet, almost forgotten, is the pause before footfall,

(Admittedly, this textual homeland, when grafted onto its historic landscape, is problematic — especially with the expansion of settlements and exclusion of "Others" with their own historical context in the landscape.) To Abrams, the "Jewish sense of exile was never merely a state of separation from a specific locale, from a particular ground; it was (and is) also a sense of separation from the very possibility of being placed, from the very possibility of being entirely at home." This displacement is, according to Abrams, "inseparable from alphabetic literacy . . . [which] can engage the human senses only to the extent that those senses sever, at least provisionally, their spontaneous participation with the animate earth."

Our alphabet, then, places a barrier between us and the natural world and our experience of place. We are displaced, sent into exile (again) as if being sent out of Eden. We feel this loss while also longing for its presence. "We long for place; but place itself longs," writes the poet Anne Michaels. (Elsewhere, Michaels says "reading a poem in translation is like kissing a woman through a veil." Nature is the poem and language the translation, the veil.) It is, as Edmund Jabès said of being Jewish, like "exiling yourself in the word and, at the same time, weeping for your exile."

So, what of the poet? If the task of the poet is to "unconceal the being of things" and words are the tools of our making, our *poeisis*, then poets need to unconceal that immediate, sensual response to nature and return us to direct contact with the land of our stories.

What this means is not a return to some original (or aboriginal) "state of nature" where human beings are displaced from our dwellings to join our fellow animals in the wilderness. Rather, a new state of nature, where humans and non-humans, and human creations, are separate but equal parts of nature. All the creations of our minds — whether

the hand about to open a door, the door ajar, a jar almost

plastic or alphabetic — are products of nature. A poem is a tree as much as the paper it is printed on.

To take this notion a bit further — reuniting our human nature with Nature, with the natural world, may allow us a path back to a unity with nature, with our natural selves. If we are nature, all we create is nature. If our creations, even our products are natural, then they, too, are of nature.

Perhaps in this reunion of human and nature, we can find the path towards healing the earth, repairing that which we have rendered separate by our distancing and dislocation. This can be achieved through dwelling.

sealed, tiny pulsating noises emanating from the seal, so

The Question of "Dwelling" & Heidegger

Dwelling — to dwell comes from the Old English *dwellan*, meaning to wander, to linger, to tarry, also to lead or go astray. It is equal to unfolding and abandonment. We inhabit our estrangement. Not inhabitation and settlement, but abandonment: leaving, leave-taking.

Habitāre has two Latin prefixes: *cohabitāre*, to dwell with another, especially in marriage or concubinage; and *inhabitāre*, to dwell in, to inhabit. To cohabit with abandonment, then, is to inhabit wandering. Resident wanderer. Resident, from the Latin *residēre*, to sit back, to stay behind, to remain, but also in Late Latin (180-600 C.E.), to sojourn (to wander?).

So, if our lot is to dwell on the earth as a wanderer, we must strive to be at home in the world, even in our wandering. We need only be rooted in our place on earth, in our abandonment, rather than a specific geographic location. Hence, the Jewish people, once transferring their history into an aleph-beth and, ultimately, into a book, were free to wander. They carried their dwelling on their backs or in a satchel or in the ark.

The question of dwelling ultimately leads to the question of Martin Heidegger — the philosopher of dwelling — and to his complicity with the Nazis. (Because this essay and its accompanying ecopoem has its origins in reaction to Heidegger's essay "Building Dwelling Thinking," we must confront this question.)

We can forgive Heidegger neither his self-serving complicity nor his silence, but even poet Paul Celan, whose parents died in the Transnistria internment camp, was compelled by Heidegger's concept of dwelling. Celan confronted Heidegger in a visit to his Black Forest peasant's dwelling in 1967 — the "Wandering Jew" meets the

small as to be almost inaudible. When is a door both

"Dweller." The Poet found his home in poiesis (making), not in any physical place. The Philosopher found his home in a dark, woody bog that came to exemplify his philosophy of dwelling. So, too, however, Celan found his dwelling, if we understand the meaning as estrangement or abandonment. (He took his own life in 1970, by drowning in the Seine.)

Celan paid attention to words. His process as a poet was, according to one translator Michael Hamburger, to take "every word as literally as possible, often breaking it down etymologically in the manner of Heidegger." Celan felt that "attention is the natural prayer of the soul." He also paid keen attention to the natural world, especially botanical details. All of which may explain why Hamburger, Jonathan Bate, and others have attempted to dissect Celan's poem "Todtnauberg," which describes the Poet's visit with Heidegger at the Philosopher's cottage, *Die Hütte*, in the Black Forest.

The poem's first word *"Arnicka"* (arnica) is an herb used to make an ointment for bruises and sprains. The second is "eyebright" or *"Augentrost"* (literally "eye-comfort"), as if the Poet is looking for some healing comfort, as eyebright is a euphrasy, used as a remedy for the eyes. In this the poet may be suggesting a "purifying water" for the "blindness" afflicting Heidegger during the Holocaust. Arnica is yellow in color, which is linked to the yellow star on a wooden block dangling above the well on Heidegger's property, which in turn is obviously linked to the yellow star the Nazis forced Jews to wear. Eyebright has white flowers with tiny yellow spots and red "veins" resembling a bloodshot eye.

(Later in the poem, the two are described as "Orchis and Orchis, walking alone." [Literally, from the Greek, "two testicles walking alone together."] The roots of *orchis masculata* supplied an energizing

opened and closed? The delay between thought and action —

68

drink called salep or salup, which was widely used before coffee was discovered, and was known as a soothing, nutritious tonic. The Arabic name for this orchid species is *Khasyu 'th-thalab* or "fox testicles." You can see why if you look at the plant from tubers to flower.)

Interpreting this poem in his book *The Song of the Earth*, Bate quotes Celan's "Conversation in the Mountains": "The Jew and Nature are strangers to each other . . . what is earthy and material is language, not ground; what is cultivated is text, not crops." In exile, the "People of the Book" were without a homeland, but this does not mean they were without a dwelling. Even the Poet Celan, who was an amateur botanist through much of his youth, knew more about the plants and animals of the Black Forest than did the Philosopher who had his dwelling there.

The complicity of Heidegger is inexcusable. So, too, is his silence on the subject after the War and his categorical denial of the Holocaust. He was known to use his home for Nazi indoctrinations in 1933. But what about his misinterpretation of dwelling? The Philosopher latched onto the meaning of dwelling as "rootedness," clearly not the state of wandering that is the word's own roots. In his poem, Celan, the wanderer, hopes Heidegger will offer "a thinker's/ word/ coming in [from?]/ the heart." Is the word the Poet seeks apology or apostasy?

Celan believed the task of the Poet was to "unconceal the being of things." Perhaps he sought out the Philosopher to unconceal the being of the Poet's people as true dwellers, as wanderers? He wanted Heidegger to abandon his former beliefs and at last admit to being a dweller himself. For dwelling he was, that is, in the Old Frisian sense of the word, *dwalin*, which means "to be in error."

Dwelling: to be in error — You are mistaken. The yellow star over

The Question of "Langscaping"

Langscaping is unconcealing the being of the landscape, of the world around us, unconcealing what is there — seen and unseen — between the past and the future. It is the topography and taxonomy of the mind through words that enact the presence of the land. This means not simply describing what one sees or representing, observing, but going beyond the temporal. Langscapes reveal through words — *logos* of landscape — unconcealing the being of things that flow like water over the land, as in a watershed.

All the trace elements collect and feed the words that make a langscape, intermingling with that which resides in the heart and mind, almost below consciousness. To bring forth that being, all the senses must be focused and sharp in order to be able to smell, taste, hear, see, and touch the earth and its unfolding and the memories that enfold the landscape.

Why not, then, make a poetry of langscape? Earth made of words, nature revealed by the words of our making. Perhaps this langscaping can help heal our longing for connection to our environment, allow us to reconnect with nature in a way that breaks down the barriers created by our language and technologies.

Language then becomes a bridge between two banks of a river. The river flows under the bridge with no concern for the bridge. We are standing on the bridge and, if we pay attention, our nets may skim a langscape off the water's surface. "Man is a bridge, not an end," wrote Robert Pogue Harrison, in *Forests: The Shadow of Civilization*. ("Man is not an end-product, maggot asserts," said poet Basil Bunting.)

Langscapes "grow rather than engineer," to use the language of emergent technologies. Through a complex dynamic of inputs

the well does not mean what you think it means, was there

and outputs, positive and negative feedback loops, reading, close observation, thinking, "networking," and writing, the poem emerges.

This is an organic poetry, using the emergent process to unconceal the being of things. "The whole is greater than the sum of its parts," and the poet is unaware of where the poem is going or how it will get there. The poem flirts with the edge of chaos and "quivers on the edge of order." This is the task of the poet, letting the poem emerge as it will, becoming the poem it wants to become.

"Poetry is the soul inaugurating a form," said poet Pierre-Jean Jouve. The form emerges as passages, sections, segments, stations, systems, documents, quotes, etc. All come together to embody a thematically linked "community." In the ecopoem, each part of the whole expands, contracts, reacts, contrasts, elucidates, explores, conflates, and explodes each other part, participating between and among each other. This is a community of *logos*.

"Without logos there is neither nature nor history," writes Robert Pogue Harrison, "which amounts to saying that there is no 'landscape'." Or, as Simon Schama writes in *Landscape and Memory*, "Landscapes are culture before they are nature; constructs of the imagination projected onto wood and water and rock."

The logos of landscape — or langscape — can be a way for the poet to explore the reciprocal participation between the human and non-human world, between our mind's perception and the earth's inhabitation. This is the poetry of dwelling. This is what makes an ecopoem.

before he bought the place, left by the previous owners. Don't

The Question of the "Ecopoem"

Poetry's landscape is an ecotone where human and natural orders meet.
— John Elder

The ecopoem should have those things in it that will bring forth truth to the reader. Earth brought forth through birdsong, recognizable trees: oaks, spruce, maple, hemlock; the spirit of bear, coyote, wolf, or big cats these hills have not seen for years. The ecopoem should furnish wildflowers for the tame to ponder and terrible storms for lovers of thunder. And when the snow comes and winter's expectation rises, the ecopoem will sing until spring.

Mountains can appear, or hills that roll and loll and calm our souls. Leaves will fall and rustle, the sounds and smells of our return to school each year as children. Rivers, too, should resound; the lakes, ponds, and the oceans as well. Then, too, the ecopoem should speak of love, or rather show it, and bring it forth for all to see. And desire. The dream of the earth is all about desire, as everything is about desire.

And familiar animals, domestic cats and dogs, a well-worn path leading to the cottage garden or city streets in the heat of summer or in the rain. Summers set by the rhythms of cicadas heard by the lake, diving off cliffs twenty feet high to deep pools of water below. The ecopoem should be a bellwether of memory, a repository saying the unsayable. It should use language to evoke the gods, or at least, our better nature.

It should also include the terrors and horrors of nature, the terrible things creatures do to each other — parasites and carnivorous plants, poisonous snakes and stink bugs. Nature — warts and everything.

The ecopoem well-executed, balances polemic with poetic language,

think about the Eyebright growing there, in the field beside

uses prose to explicate ideas, and returns to poetry when the spirit of things needs revealing.

Earth, image, word. Desire and love, all combined in one unending story the ecopoem is meant to tell, into a *presencing*, a bringing-forth, and an unconcealing of our dwelling.

Above all, the ecopoem should be about relationship: our relationship to each other and our relationship to the earth, our dwelling.

the Black Forest cottage; it doesn't mean the scales have fallen

The Question of Relationship

If we think about dwelling as our relationship to the human and non-human world in which we live, we must ask what this relationship means to us. Our relationship to the earth and our relationship to each other become paramount. Healing our relationship to the earth can come from enduring that relationship and bridging the gap between "us" and "other." Our human relationships need healing as much as does our relationship to the natural world.

As Kate Soper writes, "What is needed . . . is not so much new forms of awe and reverence of nature, but rather to extend to it some of the more painful concerns we have for ourselves." She argues that we can overcome the rupture we feel, the distance we feel from nature if we re-sensitize ourselves to "our combined separation from it and dependence upon it."

We cannot, therefore, afford to hope to live on the earth without using its resources to benefit our species. At the same time, this also means we shan't be despoilers. The question then becomes what our relationship to such use may be, what our conception of value is and what preconceptions we bring to valuing the earth.

"People who care conserve; people who don't know don't care," as Robert Michael Pyle has said. Our relationship to the non-human is formed by our preconceptions of that relationship. "What is the extinction of the condor to a child who has never known the wren?" Pyle asks. Our children live in direct relationship to their surroundings; the concept of the earth is deeply connected to home and their experience of it. A child who knows the species, non-human and human alike, of her home grows to appreciate the diversity that makes her dwelling. What this child experiences of the world further confirms her worldview, makes her world.

from the eyes. Euphrasy — he knows not of it. And if he had

If we acknowledge that human beings are a part of nature, then our relationship to nature changes. Just as our relationship to other human beings informs the parameters of those relationships, so too with our relationship to other species. Mother, father, brother, sister, uncle, aunt, grandmother, grandfather, husband, wife, lover, friend, neighbor, and stranger all have inherent parameters within which we bring-forth our relationship to each other. So too our relationships with non-human species: our relationship to domestic pets is different from our relationship to coyote, oak tree, chickadee, garden flower, and even our food sources, both plant and animal.

Then the question becomes how to define these relationships as simultaneously interconnected and separate? We feel pain when a loved one is injured or troubled. So perhaps we should allow ourselves to feel pain when the earth is injured, or a species is in trouble. Perhaps only then can our relationship to the earth and its species come to a place where we understand the parameters — our mutual separation from and dependence upon each other.

Some of these parameters are defined for us and can send false messages. The dualism between country and city fosters separation, not interdependence. Is the child growing up in the country more connected to nature by her closeness to the land? Does this have to be the case? In fact, we can't afford for this to be the case, if desensitizing to both separation and interdependence in fact leads to a lack of care. If the only way we care is to know, then we must cultivate within us a conception that wherever we dwell is a part of nature. Then may we begin to care for our dwelling.

it to do all over again, the Philosopher would have looked the

The Question of Cities & Nature

It has to be like that where everything fits — / Man into Nature, because the town is Nature. — Fernando Pessoa

If human beings are "of nature" and our making is nature brought-forth, then our cities are also products of nature. We dwell in cities. We are part of their organized complexity and, therefore, our cities are part of our "natural" environment.

If we view cities as constructs that contribute to our alienation from nature, we forget that we, like all other animals, share a reliance on the earth's environment. If, rather, we view cities as an extension of ourselves, of our dwelling or being on the earth, then cities become a part of nature too. Cities become nature because we make them, and we are part of nature. (Nature stems from the Latin *natura*, meaning birth or character. Perhaps "nature," then, is just a meme passed from one to another in English since 1662, when the word was first used to describe "the material world beyond human civilization or society" — and, coincidentally, the same year the last Dodo was sighted.)

We need to arrive at an understanding of the ecosystem of a city, as a natural construct, as dwelling. "Humanity," as Kate Soper writes, "is both the creature of nature and its creator." As such, we are "responsible for the forms of [our] interaction and in principle capable of transforming them." If there is no division between humanity and nature, then our cities are an extension of nature. This seems a more "natural," less artificial way to look at cities, especially if they are our dwelling, our way of being on the earth. We must be capable, then, of being in relationship to nature in the city. The city ecosystem can bridge the separation between humanity and nature.

Our city gardens help keep us connected to the natural world and its

other way, looked after his own skin, just as he did. Unjust

processes, if only through the daily interactions we have with tending to nature, as a tender of the garden. All our interactions in a city, in some way, connect us to the natural world and its diversity. The child connects with the rest of nature in the city even without a garden. Worms come to the surface of a sidewalk after a rain; insects crawl over our human-created habitats and find ways to adapt to and adopt them as their dwellings. Exploring the "nature" of a city park can provide as much sustenance to a child as a trip to the wilderness. Of course, wilderness offers a different kind of sustenance, a wholly different experience, both of scale and the perspective of no longer being on the top of the food chain. Although the small circle of our gardens and houses cannot hold the chaos of a city ecosystem at bay, this should not cause us concern.

This is something I call a "one square yard" philosophy: that getting to know the nature of one square yard is as important in instructing our relationship with nature as is a hike in the remote woods.

We are interacting within nature by our interactions with both human and non-human species or even within the ecosystem of our neighborhoods. But if we need daily contact with the rest of nature, non-human nature, we need to foster such experiences in our cities or wherever we live. We need to remember that "Nature" is a human construct, as is "landscape" and "wilderness" and "city." As a product of our minds, these are also constructs of nature.

"All landscapes are constructed," Anne Whiston Spirn tells us in her essay "Constructing Nature: The Legacy of Frederick Law Olmstead": "Garden, forest, and wilderness are all shaped by rivers and rain, plants and animals, human hands and minds. They are phenomena of nature and culture."

as it may seem. No matter how mistaken he may have been.

Thus, our dwelling can bridge the divide between culture and nature, between human and non-human. Is this not a bridge worth making? To view cities as an interaction between organic and inorganic constructs that are part of nature and culture, we need to let go of our assumptions concerning "otherness." Cities are constructs of our mind as well as our dwelling.

Perhaps we can tend the dwelling of our cities by thinking of building as dwelling, and promoting diversity of habitat, for both human and non-human species. Thinking about building as dwelling, we can build (or rebuild) our cities intentionally to be more conducive to and inclusive of nature, thus helping make our cities more livable, while simultaneously healing our rupture with Nature.

Dwelling: to doubt — To doubt whether all this thinking

The Question of the City as an Ecosystem

Cities are problems in organized complexity. Districts, neighborhoods, blocks, streets, and dwellings are an interrelated and integrated system, an organism, and a natural community. All its elements comprise an ecosystem.

Eco, is from the Greek *oikos*, meaning home. A home system — economy, ecology; functioning in its interconnectedness. The city is a continuous network of lively, interesting streets, where neighbors and strangers intermingle in diversity. There are clearly delineated differences between public and private space, but each are interrelated, not distinctly self-operating.

A city is an ecosystem of diverse cultures. Neighborhoods are habitats within the city ecosystem; they are an interconnected and indispensable part of the city's ecosystem. As neighborhoods become dull or lack the liveliness engendered by diversity, they sow the seeds of their own destruction. So, too, thriving neighborhoods sow the seeds of their own regeneration. What happens matters and what matters happens. Say that the energy of regeneration needs tending and fostering if cities are to survive, if they are to become our dwelling.

A shop closing on one city street affects the other shops on the block, which in turn affects the nature of the whole neighborhood, resulting, possibly, in a change in the entire district. Thus, the city evolves or devolves in a certain way. There is flux, but stability, in diversity, both human and economic. (See Jane Jacobs, *The Death and Life of Great American Cities*.)

A tree planted on a city street in the middle of a neighborhood can have more than just an effect on air quality. Others may be moved to plant trees as the feeling they get from that first tree is good, or

about dwelling will amount to much. To doubt whether

they may plant flower boxes, spruce up their garden, remove litter from the sidewalk, or somehow be moved to be kinder to their neighbors.

Suddenly, strangers appear, and they feel good in the neighborhood. Perhaps they want to become part of it, so they buy in and become neighbors, contributing to the diversity.

So, too, an abandoned dwelling falls from grace, becoming just a building. Then, as it deteriorates, the abandoned building begins to take with it other buildings or dwellings nearby. Before long, all is lost.

What happens to the integrity of an interrelated system when such a change occurs? When someone changes an architectural feature of the block or neighborhood — say, to turn a front porch into a driveway — it can create a dramatic, cascading effect. Suddenly, everyone on the block wants a driveway. Soon the porches are gone, and so is the neighborliness of the neighborhood. Perhaps tempers flare over honking horns or cars backing out of driveways. Then a carport is set up, which soon turns into a garage. Neighbors pull into their garage, park their cars, and enter their houses through interior doors, never seeing their neighbors. Thus, the neighborly character of the neighborhood is gone. A city is an ecosystem of interdependence, reliant on all its parts.

While a city may be an ecosystem, it is not isolated as such. It interacts with the ecosystems surrounding it, whether suburb, town, farm, or wildland. Like many ecosystems, indeed all ecosystems, the species within an ecosystem may be interdependent with surrounding ecosystems or habitats, even — as in the case of cities — dependent

the form is up to the questions, whether the questions

upon far-away ecosystems for clean water or food, as an example. If we think of a city as an ecosystem, tend to its ecology, and encourage its diversity, our cities may become dwelling. Bringing forth the nature of cities as dwelling may help us resist the temptation of "going back" to Nature — if that is even possible — and of viewing nature as something outside ourselves.

"It is surely not a matter of 'going back,' but rather of coming full circle," writes David Abrams. "Uniting our capacity for cool reason with those more sensorial and mimetic ways of knowing, letting the vision of a common world root itself in our direct, participating engagement with the local and particular."

If we tend to the dwelling of our cities and foster their essential nature, we can reestablish our relationship with nature wherever we dwell. This can also affect the design of our dwellings and our cities. If we turn to nature to help us solve essential design problems, we may even be able to make our cities more sustainable by reflecting — even embracing — nature through biomimicry.

unanswered, remain or rebound. To doubt whether dwelling

The Question of Biomimicry

Life has learned to fly, circumnavigate the globe, live in the depths of the ocean and atop the highest peaks, craft miracle materials, light up the night, lasso the sun's energy, and build a self-reflecting brain. Collectively, organisms have managed to turn rock and sea into a life-friendly home, with steady temperatures and smoothly percolating cycles. In short, living things have done everything we want to do, without guzzling fossil fuels, polluting the planet, or mortgaging the future. What better models could there be? — Janine Benyus

The human organism is an extremely complex feedback system. A feedback system maintains a prescribed relationship between outputs and inputs by comparing the two and using the difference to control action.

In the presence of stimulations (inputs), humans tend to reduce the difference between output and input based on the feedback from this difference.

(Think: "Learn from our mistakes . . . ")

Are human beings, then, a naturally closed-loop system? A closed-loop system adjusts its output response according to a control input

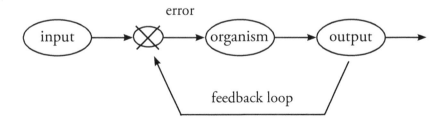

matters at all, perhaps we are like ants blindly going about

or reference and the resulting feedback. This feedback is compared to the reference to calculate an error and make corrections or adjustments.

(Think: "To err is human, to [correct] divine . . . ")

In closed-loop systems, the output has a direct impact upon the action. Feedback action is used to reduce errors.

(Think: "I'll never make that mistake again . . . ")

Natural systems produce without any wasteful byproducts. Nature, then, is a closed-loop system. Everything used to produce something in nature either goes into the end product or is eventually recycled or otherwise returned into productive relationship within the system.

(Think: "What is waste for one is food for another.")

Species have evolved ways to maximize production using limited resources and minimizing waste. Spiders, for example, produce the strongest, lightest fiber — pound for pound, five times stronger than steel — from nothing more than their food, much of which they trap in their webs made of this same fiber.

To produce the human species' strongest equivalent fiber, Kevlar, we need extremely high temperatures, petroleum-based raw materials, sulfuric acid, and massive amounts of energy, resulting in extremely toxic byproducts that are not recoverable within our ecosystems.

What is the logic in this construct? There are errors in need of feedback corrections.

our business, and it is better not to question. Assuming

Biomimicry is the process of observing nature and using its close-looped systems to improve design.

(Think: "What is good for the goose . . . ")

Biomimicry can improve our designs (outputs) and reduce our negative impacts (errors).

(Think: "The error of our ways . . . ")

In a way, we already are biomimics: barbs on burr seeds inspired Velcro, etc. The way plants self-clean their leaves inspired self-cleaning paints. The way marshes filter organic waste inspired wastewater treatment plants that recover usable water.

Closed-loop products are recycled within the system, mimicking nature's processes.

(Think: "One company's waste is another company's raw material.")

Yet, through hubris, human beings discarded biomimicry in favor of our own ingenuity and engineering, ignoring the errors surfaced by our own feedback loops.

The way vulture wings inspired the wing design of the Wright brothers. The way Alaskan hunters observe and mimic polar bears to catch seals. The way ravens help guide hunters — wolves and humans — to easy prey.

Nature's logic has evolved from four billion years of experience and adaptation to create resilient, adaptive, sustainable systems.

we   have   a   purpose   at   all,   what   is   dwelling?   It   will   be

(Say that using nature's logic is a way of knowing.)

Biomimicry can serve as a bridge over our separation from nature.

(Say that a bridge connects more than the banks of a river.)

We can use biomimicry, then, to unconceal the being of our dwelling, to reveal the essence of *home*.

enough if all this thinking about dwelling is worthy of

The Question of Dwelling (Home)

Gaston Bachelard said, "There exists for each one of us an oneiric house, a house of dream-memory, that is lost in the shadow beyond the real past." What is our home and how do we make it? How do we bring it forth (*poeisis*) out of the shadows and into the light of presence?

Home is a house made of breath, as William Goyen would have it, "founded on the most fragile web of breath and you had blown it . . . an idea of breath breathed out by you who, with that same breath that had blown it, could blow it all away."

So, home is in the shadows of our dream-memory and in our breath. Home is an idea that consists of all the memories we have and all that we have forgotten. "Our soul is an abode," according to Bachelard.

Home is an apartment, a house on a city block, a country estate, a cottage, a cabin, a condo, a room, a tent, or even a nest. "Intimacy needs the heart of a nest." We carry home within us along with all the stories of our culture that tell us who we are. While we may never find our home in the physical sense, it may inhabit us, and we will never lose it.

Once we find a house we try to make it a home by shaping the space to meet our idea (ideal?) of home. We surround ourselves with things that conjure memories: paintings, photographs, books, music, food, furniture, tchotchkes, maybe a garden, a porch with a glider or rocking chairs, windows looking out on the street or the horizon, the rooms of our nesting, people, things with special meaning or association.

Home is dwelling. Home is from the Old English *hām*, which means "house with land." Other origins link it to world, village, family. In

questioning and thereby worthy of thought — Doubt,

Sanskrit, the closest word to home, *kayati*, means "he is lying down." In Greek, it is *keitai*, "he is recumbent." Thus, home is the place where we lie down.

Dwelling is the being of home, its presence and its essence. As such, it haunts us. ("To haunt" is *hanter* in Old French or *hanten* in Middle English.) Home or the idea of home haunts us, especially if—like Odysseus—we are always searching for it, for the way "back home." All we can do is try to make it, try to bring forth home as dwelling.

Perhaps all this thinking about dwelling, about the being (existence) or essence of home will only succeed in planting seeds for thinking about how we live on the earth. "Enough will have been gained if dwelling . . . " as Heidegger wrote, has "become worthy of questioning and thus [has] remained worthy of thought."

the Philosopher says, is the privilege of the faithful.

Works Cited

Abrams, David. *The Spell of the Sensuous: Perception and Language in the More-Than-Human World*. New York: Vintage Books, 1997.

Bachelard, Gaston. *The Poetics of Space*. Translated by Maria Jolas and Joseph R. Stilgoe. Boston: Beacon Press, 1994.

Bate, Jonathan. *The Song of the Earth*. London: Picador, 2000.

Benyus, Janine. *Biomimicry: Innovation Inspired by Nature*. New York: HarperCollins, 2002.

Berry, Thomas. *Dream of the Earth*. San Francisco: Sierra Club Books, 1990.

Bidart, Frank. *In the Western Night: Collected Poems, 1965-1990*. New York: Farrar, Straus & Giroux, 1990.

Bishop, Elizabeth. *The Complete Poems: 1927-1979*. New York: Farrar, Straus & Giroux, 1983.

Bunting, Basil. *Collected Poems*. Mt. Kisco: Moyer Bell Ltd., 1995.

Calvino, Italo. *The Baron in the Trees*. Translated by Archibald Colquhoun. New York: Harcourt Brace Jovanovich, 1977.

Carson, Anne. *Eros the Bittersweet*. Champaign: Dalkey Archive Press, 1986.

Celan, Paul. *Poems of Paul Celan*. Translated by Michael Hamburger. New York: Persea Books, 1988.

Chomsky, Noam. *Cartesian Linguistics: A Chapter in the History of Rationalist Thought*. New York: Harper & Row, 1966.

Clare, John. *"I Am": The Selected Poetry of John Clare*. Edited by Jonathan Bate. New York: MacMillan, 2003.

Elder, John. *Imagining the Earth: Poetry and the Vision of Nature*. Athens: The University of Georgia Press, 1996.

Erasmus, Desiderius. *The Erasmus Reader*. Edited by Erika Rummel. Toronto: The University of Toronto Press, 1990.

Goyen, William. *House of Breath*. New York: Random House, 1950.

Harrison, Robert Pogue. *Forests: The Shadow of Civilization*. Chicago: The University of Chicago Press, 1992.

Heidegger, Martin. "The Question Concerning Technology," *Basic Writings*. Edited by David Farrell Krell. New York: Harper & Row, 1977.

Heidegger, Martin. "Building Dwelling Thinking." *Poetry, Language, Thought*. Translated by Albert Hofstadter. New York: Harper Colophon Books, 1971.

Hölderlin, Friedrich. *Poems and Fragments*. Translated by Michael Hamburger. Ann Arbor: The University of Michigan Press, 1966.

Homer. *The Odyssey*. Translated by Robert Fagles. New York: Viking Press, 1996.

Jacobs, Jane. *The Death and Life of Great American Cities*. New York: Vintage Books, 1989.

Jabès, Edmond. *The Book of Questions*. Translated by Keith Waldrop. Middletown: Wesleyan University Press, 1987.

Meadows, Donella, Dennis Meadows, and Jørgen Randers. *Beyond the Limits: Confronting Global Collapse, Envisioning Sustainable Future*. Chelsea: Chelsea Green Publishing, 1992.

Merleau-Ponty, Maurice. *The Visible and the Invisible*. Translated by Alphonso Lingus. Evanston: Northwestern University Press, 1968.

Michaels, Anne. *Fugitive Pieces*. New York: Vintage Books, 1998.

Mitchell, Susan. *Erotikon: Poems*. New York: HarperCollins, 2000.

Morgenstern, Joseph. "The Gehry Style," *New York Times Magazine*, 16 May 1982.

Pamuk, Orhan. *Snow*. Translated by Maureen Freely. New York: Knopf, 2004.

Paz, Octavio. *Labyrinth of Solitude and Other Writings*. Translated by Lysander Kemp, Yara Milos, and Rachel Phillips Belash. New York: Grove Press, 1985.

Paz, Octavio. *The Collected Poems of Octavio Paz, 1957–1987*. Translated by Elliot Weinberger, et al. New York: New Directions Publishing, 1991.

Pessoa, Fernando. *Poems of Fernando Pessoa*. Translated and edited by Edwin Honig and Susan M. Brown. New York: The Ecco Press, 1986.

Pyle, Robert Michael. *The Thunder Tree: Lessons from an Urban Wildland*. New York: The Lyons Press, 1998.

Schama, Simon. *Landscape and Memory*. New York: A. A. Knopf, 1995.

Snyder, Gary. *Turtle Island*. New York: New Directions Publishing, 1974.

Soper, Kate. *What is Nature?: Culture, Politics and the non-Human*. Oxford: Blackwell Publishers, 1995.

Spirn, Anne Whiston. "Constructing Nature: The Legacy of Frederick Law Olmstead." In *Uncommon Ground: Rethinking the Human Place in Nature*, edited by William Cronon. New York: W. W. Norton, 1995.

Stevens, Wallace. *The Collected Poems of Wallace Stevens*. New York: Knopf, 1954.

Suzuki, David, with Amanda McConnell and Adrienne Mason. *The Sacred Balance: Rediscovering Our Place in Nature*. Vancouver: Greystone Books, 2002.

Wordsworth, William. *The Prelude: The Four Texts*. Edited by Jonathan Wordsworth. London: Penguin Books, 1995.

About the Author

Photo: Samantha Anderson, 2017

Scott Edward Anderson is the author of *Fallow Field* (Aldrich Press, 2013) and *Walks in Nature's Empire* (The Countryman Press, 1995). He has been a Concordia Fellow at the Millay Colony for the Arts and received the *Nebraska Review* Award. His work has appeared in the *American Poetry Review, Alaska Quarterly Review, Cimarron Review, The Cortland Review, Many Mountains Moving, Terrain,* and the anthologies *Dogs Singing* (Salmon Poetry, 2011) and *The Incredible Sestina Anthology* (Write Bloody, 2013), among other publications.

Anderson founded TheGreenSkeptic.com, which he wrote for ten years, worked for The Nature Conservancy from 1992-2007, and currently consults with conservation organizations and cleantech companies. He lives in Brooklyn, New York, with his wife, Samantha, and their blended family. Learn more about his work at ScottEdwardAnderson.com and connect with him on Twitter @greenskeptic.

SHANTI ARTS

nature · art · spirit

Please visit us on online

to browse our entire book catalog,

including additional poetry collections and fiction,

books on travel, nature, healing, art,

photography, and more.

shantiarts.com